Devon Railw Stations

on old picture postcards

Part One: The Great Western Railway

Andrew Swift

St. David's Station, Exeter

1. Gateway to Devon. A curiously deserted view of **Exeter St David's** as it looked around 1905. Despite being a long way from the city centre, it has remained Exeter's principal station ever since it opened in 1846. It looks very different today yet still breathes much of the spirit of the old GWR - and of the LSWR, whose trains were grudgingly allowed to call there en route to the far west. *(Postcard published by Valentine of Dundee)*

£3.50

Introduction

For many people the Great Western *was* Devon. The most famous stretch of railway in Britain was the few miles along the sea wall from Dawlish Warren to Teignmouth, with the red cliffs of Devon towering above.

The Great Western's Publicity Department exploited the natural charms of the county to the full, creating an image of Torbay as a holiday destination to rival the South of France. It is an image that still survives. The line along the sea wall survives as well. Although copper-capped engines no longer tear along, shovelling steam over their shoulder, there is still a sense of magic as today's high-speed trains roar past Compton Cove and Langstone Rock, their two-tone horns echoing off the cliffs.

And the old Great Western line is still the most dramatic way to enter Devon. Climbing from Taunton, it plunges, still in Somerset, into the blackness of Whiteball Tunnel, before crossing the county boundary to emerge in Devon. A few miles further on, it drops into the broad valley of the River Culm, its lush pastures broken here and there by ploughed fields of an almost implausible redness, for the run down to Exeter.

The Great Western in Devon had another face, however. From junctions all along the main line, slow, single-track branches ran inland, along deep, wooded valleys, to quiet market towns by the side of broad estuaries or high into the foothills of the moors. There was even a line that curled up onto Dartmoor to reach England's highest station. Today all that is left of this network of lines is the preserved Dart Valley Railway, a museum piece to give us a glimpse of what we have lost.

The Western Region of British Railways, which took over the Great Western's lines after nationalisation in 1948, was particularly vehement - and particularly quick off the mark - in its closure programme. The name of Dr Beeching is held as anathema by railway lovers today, but many of the lines and stations in this book closed long before he came on the scene. Sizeable towns like Plympton and Cullompton lost their stations, even though trains still continued to run through them. Tiverton, the largest town in mid-Devon, once served by two branch lines, lost its station because no attempt was made to make its services more attractive to passengers. Today there are plans to undo some of the damage done in the 1950's and 1960's but most of the stations that closed will never see a train again. Many of them had run out of steam years before the trains stopped calling, underused and almost forgotten by the communities they were built to serve. They belonged to an age when the only alternative to the train was the horse and cart - or Shanks's pony.

Some, though, were closed needlessly. Although railways will never again enjoy the monopoly they had when the postcards in this book were published, they still have a vital role to play. So, as well as nostalgia for a vanished age, I hope that the pictures that follow may provide some inspiration for the future.

Andrew Swift
June 2001

2. The GWR's other station in **Exeter, St Thomas,** is just under a mile south of St David's. It has always been well patronised, yet was closed as a wartime economy measure from April 1917 to March 1919. The platform on the left was lengthened in 1930 and the overall roof demolished in 1971. However, the Italianate buildings designed by Brunel still survive. *(JB Sherlock)*

3. Stoke Canon was three miles north of Exeter St David's on the main line to Taunton. On this card from around 1905, the main line can be seen curving round to the right, while the Exe Valley branch forks off to the left. This station opened in 1894 to replace an earlier station north of the junction. It was rebuilt in 1931, when the track through the station was quadrupled, and closed to passengers in 1960. *(GW Southerden)*

4. Four miles along the Culm Valley from Stoke Canon was the wayside station of **Silverton**, with its platforms staggered on either side of a road overbridge. The wide gap between the running lines is a reminder that they were originally built to the GWR's broad gauge (7ft and a quarter inch) before conversion to standard gauge (4ft 8 and a half inches) in 1892. This isolated station, with its elaborate bargeboards and well-stocked flower-beds, was over two miles from the village it served. It opened in 1867 and closed to passengers in 1964.

5. A few miles further along the Culm Valley line, the historic wool town of **Cullompton** merited - and got - an altogether more well-appointed station. On this view sent from the town in 1913 the imposing covered footbridge effectively hides the buildings from view. Cullompton station, dating from 1844, was extensively rebuilt in 1931 when the track through it was quadrupled. Its closure in 1964 still seems like an act of wilful perversity and reopening has been proposed as part of the County Structure Plan.
(A. Haley, Cullompton)

I intend coming to your nice little service at Langford soon.

AUTO-FOTO CO'S. DEVON SERIES   No. 22 TIVERTON JUNCTION, WILLAND.   PTD. IN ENGLAND.

6. Tiverton Junction, two miles north of Cullompton, opened in 1844 and was known as Tiverton Road until a branch opened to Tiverton four years later. It survived the closure of both the Tiverton branch and the other intermediate stations between Exeter and Taunton in the 1960's, finally succumbing in 1986 when a new station, Tiverton Parkway, opened two miles to the north. The view on this card, posted from Exeter in July 1905, shows the station from the west, with the Tiverton branch trailing in the foreground.   *(Auto-Foto Co.)*

Tiverton Station   E 31966

7. The impressive station at **Tiverton** dates from 1885, replacing an earlier one built in 1848. Elaborate bargeboards, footbridge towers reminiscent of those at Torquay (although with gable ends) and three gables punctuating the roof-line added up to a station worthy of the most important town in mid-Devon. As well as a shuttle service to Tiverton Junction, four and a half miles away, Tiverton was served by trains on the Exe Valley branch from Exeter to Dulverton. It should never have closed, but after the inevitable rundown the last passenger trains ran on 5 October 1964. Goods traffic ended three years later. *(Stengel & Co.)*

8. Four miles south of Exeter St Thomas was **Exminster**, the only station between Exeter and Newton Abbot to have closed - in 1964. The Italianate stucco building designed by Brunel can be seen on the left. The station was extensively remodelled in the 1920's and 1930's, and the track through it quadrupled.

9. A distant view of the waterside station at **Starcross**, opened in 1846, from where passengers could catch a ferry to Exmouth. Just south of the station is a massive pumping house, legacy of Brunel's "atmospheric railway." These were built at intervals along the line to create a vacuum in a tube between the rails. This sucked trains along on a principle similar to that once used in department stores to whisk money to a central cash desk. So many maintenance problems were encountered, however, that it was soon abandoned. *(Chapmans of Dawlish)*

10. The most famous stretch of railway line in the country is the four and a half mile run along the sea wall from Dawlish Warren to Teignmouth. In this view of the station at **Dawlish,** the line can be seen disappearing into the distance. It is a pity that this dignified Regency resort lost its sea front and its seclusion thanks to Brunel's determination to drive his railway along the coast rather than seek an inland route (imagine Lyme Regis, a similar resort to Dawlish, with a railway running along its sea front), but at least the glorious ride along the coast is some recompense. *(Chapmans of Dawlish)*

11. An idea of the problems faced by Brunel in building his sea-wall railway - and of today's Railtrack engineers in maintaining it - can be gained from this card showing waves crashing over **Dawlish** station. Despite its fame, most visitors to Devon never take a trip along the sea wall. Marketing of it as a top tourist and heritage attraction - with express steam shuttle services - could draw in thousands of visitors a year, but the current GWR seems to have lost its illustrious predecessor's magical touch for marketing.

12. Dawlish Warren opened in 1912 with platform loops to allow expresses to overtake local trains. It was intended primarily for summer visitors and had a basic set of wooden buildings with no platform canopy. It closed as a wartime economy measure from January 1917 to May 1919 but is still open today. This card of a local train for Exeter pulling into the station was published shortly after it opened. *(Chapmans of Dawlish)*

13. Before Dawlish Warren station opened, the area was served by **Warren Platform**, with its two pagoda-style shelters, a quarter of a mile to the south. It opened in 1905 and proved so popular that it only lasted seven years before being replaced by the present station. Here a steam railmotor for Teignmouth calls at Warren Platform as a train for Exeter pulls away in the other direction.

Newton Abbot, Great Western Station.

14. Newton Abbot - originally plain Newton - was not only the point at which the Torbay branch left the main line, it was also the start of the switchback gradients that took the main line over the foothills of Dartmoor to Plymouth. The station, originally opened in 1846, was completely rebuilt in the mid-1920's, when this pseudo-Palladian building, its central pediment flanked by an extraordinary non-balustraded mansard roof, was added. *(Frith)*

Newton Abbot Junction.

15. The road bridge to the south of **Newton Abbot** station remains one of the best places in Devon to watch the railway at work. In the days of steam, when Newton Abbot shed was one of the busiest on the system, it must have been endlessly fascinating. On this card from around 1905, the old station with its overall roof, swept away in the 1920's, can be seen in the background. *(J Welch, Portsmouth)*

16. A train calls at **Brent**, junction for Kingsbridge, with the foothills of Dartmoor in the background. This card shows the GWR in Devon at its best - expansive, confident and surrounded by magnificent scenery. Brent station opened in 1848 and closed in 1964, although reopening has been suggested as part of the County Structure Plan. *(WR Gay)*

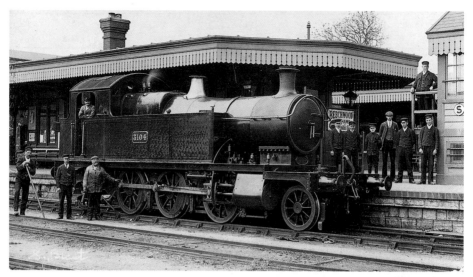

17. An engine standing at the Kingsbridge branch platform at **Brent**. No less than eleven railway workers appear on this card, but overstaffing like this was no problem when the quarter of a million men who worked on the railways earned an average of only 25s10d a week each (roughly £65 in today's terms). Two-fifths of them - including no doubt the junior staff in this picture - earned less than £1 a week (equal to around £50 today). Pictures like this may conjure up a lost age, but for many people at the time - including those who worked on the railways - life was far from the Edwardian idyll we sometimes imagine. *(WR Gay)*

18. A distant view of **Totnes** which shows not only the pumping house erected by Brunel for his ill-fated atmospheric system, but also the train sheds which extended out from each platform and were later removed. Totnes station dates from 1847.

19. Ivybridge, the GWR country station par excellence, with the foothills of Dartmoor in the background. It opened in 1848 and closed to passengers in 1959. The wooden Italianate station building on the left-hand platform is hidden by the footbridge. A new station opened at Ivybridge in 1994.

20. Another view of **Ivybridge** station showing a train from Exeter crossing the viaduct over the wooded valley of the River Erme. The viaduct was built by Sir James Inglis in 1893 to replace the wooden one built by Brunel. Note also the mixed goods train in the siding on the right. Goods receipts outweighed passenger receipts at most stations in Devon. It was the steady drift of freight away from the railways after the Second World War which was largely responsible for the sweeping closure programmes of the 1950's and 1960's. This card was posted from Torquay on 13 August 1914. *(Valentines of Dundee)*

21. A lively scene at **Cornwood** station, two and a half miles west of Ivybridge and high in the valley of the River Yealm, as a Plymouth-bound train pulls in. This station, amazingly elaborate for a village of 1,000 people, opened in 1852 and closed to passengers in 1959. This card was published around 1910. *(WR Gay)*

The Station, Plympton.

22. Plympton, four miles east of Plymouth, opened in 1848 and closed to passengers in 1959 despite serving a large and growing town. Reopening (local residents have been campaigning for this for years), is now a serious possibility, having been enshrined in the County Structure Plan. *(Charles Tucker, Plympton)*

23. The GWR idea of the basic station is exemplified by this view of the wooden platforms at **Laira Halt**, one and a half miles east of Plymouth (North Road). It opened in 1904 and closed in 1930. The name of Laira is well-known to railway enthusiasts as the location of Plymouth's rail depot.

24. Mutley, just over a mile east of the old GWR Plymouth terminus at Millbay, opened in 1871 to serve the residential area north of the city. However, only six years later the GWR and LSWR opened a joint station at North Road, a third of a mile west of Mutley, which soon became the city's principal station. Despite this, Mutley continued to be well patronised - as can be seen from this card from around 1914 - until it closed in 1939. Mutley's situation at the mouth of a tunnel, with houses climbing the banks on either side of the line, is reminiscent of the western exit from Newport in Monmouthshire.   *(Harding, Bristol)*

25. A train at **Plymouth (North Road)**, opened jointly by the GWR and LSWR in 1877 and now Plymouth's principal station. This locomotive, "Albany," was one of 156 "Bulldog" class locomotives built at Swindon to a design by William Dean between 1899 and 1910. None have survived into preservation.

26. The South Devon Railway opened its terminus at **Plymouth (Millbay)** in 1849. The arrival of the railway made Millbay Docks, opened nine years earlier, a main point of arrival for ocean-going liners. This postcard shows the interior of the station early last century. Although well-situated for the city centre, once the Tamar bridge opened and trains began running to Cornwall, the need to reverse at Millbay created difficulties and delays. In 1877 a joint station was opened with the LSWR at North Road which Cornwall-bound trains could call at without reversing. From that point on Millbay began a period of decline which ended with closure to passengers in 1941 after it suffered bomb damage. *(JB Sherlock)*

27. This view of **Plymouth (Millbay)**, with its expansive porte-cochere, is dominated by the Duke of Cornwall Hotel - Victorian Gothic at its most cluttered and intimidating - built by Foster Hayward in 1865. Gothic hotels were all the rage in the 1860's. As well as the Duke of Cornwall, there was CW Horne's Ilfracombe Hotel (1863), JP Seddons' Aberystwyth Hotel, which became the University College (1864), and George Gilbert Scott's St Pancras Hotel (1865). *(WH Smith)*

THE STATION, IDE

28. Compared with the overblown fancy of the Duke of Cornwall Hotel, the lack of anything approaching architectural pretension in this view of **Ide** station comes as a welcome relief. Ide was a couple of miles out of Exeter on a line which opened in 1903 to link up with the Teign Valley Railway at Christow. This card was sent from nearby Alphington in April 1907 with the cryptic message: *"Rained again yesterday, roll on Saturday."* Ide station closed in 1958.

29. Christow opened in 1903 when the Teign Valley branch was extended to Exeter. A
high on Dartmoor. It would have been a splendid line, but closed, as those to Moret
to goods in 1961.   *(Chapmans of Dawlish)*

CHRISTOW 7479

time there were plans to extend the line from here along the Teign Valley to Chagford,
pstead and Princetown did, in the 1950's. Christow closed to passengers in 1958 and

30. *"This is our station . . . not much fear of getting lost"* reads the message on the back of this card of **Ashton**, the original terminus of the Teign Valley Railway, postmarked August 1913. The Teign Valley line served a string of villages in the glorious and little-known countryside south-west of Exeter. Just occasionally, when the sea breached the main line near Dawlish, passengers on the Torbay Express would get to see it as their train wound slowly down the branch. Ashton closed to passengers in 1958 and today, when the sea wall collapses, passengers have to go by bus. *(Chapmans of Dawlish)*

31. Trusham opened in 1882 when a branch was opened from Heathfield, on the Moretonhampstead branch, to Ashton. This card was sent from Trusham in 1916. This was the archetypal wayside station - a single platform, a basic brick building with waiting room and offices, a corrugated iron hut and a signal box. Trusham, which later acquired a passing loop, closed to passengers in 1958. *(Chapmans of Dawlish)*

32. This card shows the scene at **Chudleigh** on the Teign Valley branch as an Exeter-bound train arrives. Although this picture dates from around 1910, you could have returned in the mid-1950's and found the scene virtually unchanged. The clothes, the posters, the engine and the coaches would have been different, but in its essentials it would have been the same. Yet all around it, things had moved on. Buses, cars and lorries had destroyed the railways' monopoly. They were, in most cases, cheaper, quicker, and more convenient, and the railways did nothing about it. It is unlikely that stations like Chudleigh could have survived, but the sad thing is that nobody even tried to save them. *(Chapmans of Dawlish)*

33. Kingskerswell, on the Torbay branch, opened in 1853 and closed, incomprehensibly, in 1964. It served a growing commuter area then, and many of the trains that continued to pass through called at all stations between Paignton and Exeter. However, it seems that common sense may belatedly prevail, as the possibility of its reopening is mooted in the Devon County Structure Plan. *(D Murray, Teignmouth)*

34. From 1848 until the line was extended in 1859, **Torre** was Torquay's only station. It was enlarged in 1882 and provides a good example of mid and late nineteenth-century GWR design. This card unfortunately features rather more platform than anything else.   *(JB Sherlock)*

Torquay Station.   E 31290

35. The railway reached **Torquay** in 1859. In 1878 the original station was rebuilt in a style which, although not ostentatious, makes its presence felt by the splendid towers at either end of the footbridge. On this card from around 1905 note the small wagon turntable to the right of the signal. *(Stengel & Co.)*

G. W. Railway Station, Paignton.

36. *"It is very hot here. I am simply sizzled."* The message on the back of this card of **Paignton** station, sent from the town in 1911, puts all those pictures of fashionable Edwardians dressed up to the nines at the seaside into perspective. Paignton station opened in 1859. Today it is busier than ever as the junction for the Torbay Steam Railway. *(J Welch, Portsmouth)*

CHURSTON STATION.

37. In 1861 the railway was extended from Paignton to Brixham Road, which changed its name to **Churston** when a branch opened to Brixham in 1868. To the left is the platform for Brixham trains, with the main platforms on the right. This card was sent from Brixham in August 1953. Today Churston is the crossing point for trains on the Torbay Steam Railway. *(A Martin, Galmpton Post Office)*

38. Beyond Churston, the line entered a tunnel to emerge high above the valley of the River Dart. From there it ran down to **Kingswear**, which was linked with Dartmouth by ferry. The timber-built station at Kingswear opened in 1864 and was for many years the terminus of expresses from Paddington. When British Rail decided to cut its services back to Paignton in 1971, the Dart Valley Railway Company took over the Paignton-Kingswear line and renamed it the Torbay Steam Railway. Kingswear station featured memorably in the film of *The French Lieutenant's Woman*.

39. Brixham opened in 1868, the terminus of a short branch from Churston. The station was high above the town and, although passenger traffic was thin, fish traffic kept the station busy right up until closure in 1963.

40. A wonderfully off-beat card of the station at **Yealmpton**. This branch must have been a delight, winding its way down Coffleete Creek and along the lower reaches of the River Yealm to a sleepy terminus in a wooded valley. It closed to passengers in 1930 but reopened from 1941 to 1947 to cater for people who had moved out of Plymouth during the war. On this card, posted from Bigbury in April 1912, the bus for Bigbury-on-Sea stands in the station yard.

41. Shaugh Bridge Halt opened in 1907. Facilities were spartan - a couple of seats, a small pagoda-like shelter - yet the platform was surprisingly extensive. It needed to be. In the early days of the halt's existence, special trains ran non-stop from Plymouth to Shaugh Bridge on Bank Holidays, packed with thousands of day-trippers bound for Bickleigh Vale. It closed, its glory days long behind it, in 1962. *(Derry Chapman. Plymouth)*

42. The spacious station at **Yelverton**, where Plymouth-Launceston trains connected with those to Princetown. It had many peculiar features, not least the deferral of its opening until 1885, two years after the Princetown branch opened. While it was being built, Princetown trains had to run to and from Horrabridge, a mile and a half down the line. It closed in 1962.

PROWSE'S CROSSING, DOUSLAND.

43. Prowse's Crossing was just past **Dousland**, originally the only intermediate station on the Princetown branch. The signalbox controlling the crossing, and Dousland station's goods siding can be seen behind the trees. It must have been a quiet life working as a signalman at a place like this.

44. The Princetown branch was one of the most spectacular lines in the country. It rose 950 feet in ten and a half miles, at one point swinging round a two and a half mile horseshoe curve to cover just 200 yards. The isolated halt at **Ingra Tor**, with its famous sign warning dog owners of the danger of snakes, opened in 1936. Awe-inspiring on a summer's day, a journey on this line must have been hair-raising on a howling winter's night, especially if the only other person in the carriage was an unshaven and rather desperate looking man who happened to stumble aboard at a place like this. *(RS Carpenter)*

S 11342   PRINCETOWN STATION, G. W. RLY. DARTMOOR

45. Princetown owed its existence to Sir Thomas Tyrwhitt, who opened quarries and later persuaded the Admiralty to build a prison for Napoleonic prisoners of war here. In the 1820's he built a 4ft 6in horse-drawn tramway to carry granite down to the Plym estuary. The ten and a half mile branch from Yelverton to Princetown, which opened in 1883, followed the course of the tramway fairly closely. On this card a train pulls out of Princetown - at 1,373 feet above sea level the highest station in England - for a trip down to Yelverton.*(WH Smith)*

Princetown Railway Station

46. A distant view of **Princetown** station. Had the Princetown branch survived, it would be one of the great railway journeys of the world. Sadly it closed in 1956, and no trace of Princetown station now remains. Reopening is not, at present, even a remote possibility, but who knows what future generations will make of the abandoned trackbed over the moor. *(Valentine of Dundee)*

47. A Plymouth-bound train curves into the wooden station at **Horrabridge**, one and a half miles north of Yelverton and high above the Walkham Valley. From 1883 until 1885, when the station at Yelverton opened, this was the junction for the Princetown branch. Note the gap between the rails - a clear indication that the line was originally broad gauge. From 1874, when the LSWR extended their line from Exeter to Lydford, to 1890, when they got their own route from Lydford to Plymouth, LSWR trains travelled down this line to reach Plymouth.

48. The wayside station at **Coryton** in the Lyd Valley, four and a half miles west of Lydford, which opened in 1865 and closed in 1962. There were once scores of GWR wayside stations like this all over Devon - so common that nobody gave them a second thought. And then, in the space of less than ten years, every one of them closed. Today the only place in the county you can see anything remotely like the view on this card is at Staverton on the Dart Valley Railway. *(AR Kingdom)*

49. Liddaton Halt, three miles west of Lydford, opened in 1938. Although the GWR were already using concrete to build similar halts by this time, at Liddaton they opted for wood. This isolated halt served a scattered community of cottages and farms and closed when passenger services were withdrawn between Plymouth and Launceston in 1962. *(Chapmans of Dawlish)*

50. Loads of interest in this distant view of the two-platform station at **Lifton**. A goods train pulls away in the direction of Lydford, while the Ambrosia factory - its sidings filled with more wagons - steams away in the background. The station, which closed to passengers in 1962 and to goods in 1966, may not be familiar to many people but the road on the left - now the A30 - may well be. *(Chapmans of Dawlish)*

51. Teigngrace was two miles up the Moretonhampstead branch from the busy station at Newton Abbot and could not have provided a greater contrast with it. After the Moretonhampstead branch closed to passengers in 1959, a preservation society took over Teigngrace station as a base for reopening the line. They ran several specials up the branch, which was still open for goods traffic, but eventually threw in their lot with the Dart Valley Preservation Society at Buckfastleigh. *(JB Sherlock)*

G. W. Railway Station. Bovey Tracey. Chapman & Son, Dawlish

52. An early printed card showing the stone-built station at **Bovey** on the Moretonhampstead branch. Part of the line between Teigngrace and Bovey was built along the trackbed of the Haytor Granite Tramway - Devon's first railway - which opened in 1820. Granite was not only the principal traffic of this tramway but was also used for the rails. Bovey opened in 1866 and closed to passengers in 1959. Goods traffic ceased in 1970. *(Chapmans of Dawlish)*

53. Lustleigh may sound as though it belongs in *Cold Comfort Farm* but it was actually one stop down the line from Moretonhampstead. Here, on a superb panoramic card, a train for Moretonhampstead calls briefly at the one-platform station around 1910. With only five or six trains a day each way, the staff at stations like this had plenty of time to spend on gardening. They may have been an incidental aspect of the railway scene, but station gardens, now almost entirely a thing of the past, are one of the things people remember most fondly about railway journeys years ago.*(Chapmans of Dawlish)*

MORETONHAMPSTEAD 10670

54. **Moretonhampstead**, with its wooden train shed sheltering trains and passengers from the worst of the Dartmoor weather, was an archetypal GWR branch terminus. It could never have been economic to keep the 12 mile branch from Newton Abbot open once buses and lorries appeared, but a trip along it on a summer's afternoon, with hardly another passenger to disturb the tranquility, must have been a rare experience. It closed to passengers in 1959. *(Chapmans of Dawlish)*

55. Steam billows from a Victorian tank engine at **Avonwick** station deep in the Avon Valley. Avonwick was the first station out of Brent on the branch to Kingsbridge which opened in 1893 and closed in 1963. Attempts to reopen the branch as the "Primrose Line" came to nothing when British Railways sent in contractors to rip up the track. *(WR Gay)*

56. Gara Bridge was the next station down the Avon Valley line. It was here that the GWR put one of their first camping coaches. Gara Bridge was, like many Devon stations, in the middle of nowhere. The cattle pens in the goods yard, however, give a clue as to why the GWR opened a station here. Goods and livestock traffic were the mainstay of most rural stations, and when road hauliers poached them, the stations had little reason to stay open.*(WR Gay)*

57. *"This is our station. I daresay Clarrie knows it. It is rough and cold weather,"* reads the message on this card sent from Woodleigh in January 1907. **Loddiswell** station was deep in the Avon Valley, the village it served high on a nearby hill. It is hard to think of a more perfect spot for a station or - in an age of cars and buses - a more pointless one. Today the station has been immaculately restored as a private house where sometimes, on summer weekends, the owners serve cream teas on the old platform. *(WR Gay)*

58. Road-rail interchange at **Kingsbridge** in the days when - unless it travelled by train - nothing went faster than the fastest horse. The stone-built station at Kingsbridge opened in 1893 and closed a mere 70 years later in 1963. No attempt was made to make trains more attractive to passengers as buses and cars took their business away. Most trains only went as far as the junction at Brent and none ran through to Plymouth. Now in summer, with the narrow roads of the South Hams clogged with traffic, you cannot help feeling that a priceless resource was flung needlessly away. *(Stengel & Co.)*

59. The GWR was generally none too keen on vegetation on its buildings, so this view of **Brampford Speke** from around 1906 is something of a surprise. This wayside station on the Exe Valley line was less than a mile north of the junction with the main line at Stoke Canon. In 1914 the stationmaster here earned a paltry 27 shillings a week - roughly equivalent to an annual wage of around £3,500 today. With salaries like that, it is no wonder the GWR did not need to worry about overstaffing.

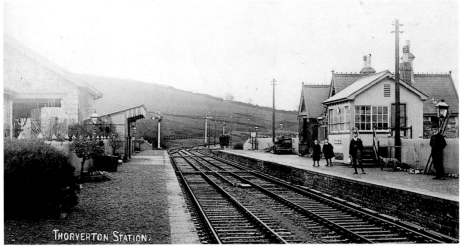

THORVERTON STATION.

60. Two miles further along the Exe Valley line came **Thorverton**, its main building, like that at Brampford Speke, following a pattern established on the Bristol & Exeter Railway in the 1840's. It opened in 1885 and closed to passengers in 1963.

Uffculme Station

G. Crease, Photo., Uffc

61. This card of **Uffculme** station sums up the character of the GWR's most curious byway in Devon. The line from Tiverton Junction to Hemyock was opened by the Culm Valley Light Railway Company in 1876. Four years later, disillusioned by lack of business, the company sold it to the GWR for £33,000. It was pure Heath Robinson. Even as late as 1963, when it closed to passengers, trains still took almost an hour to cover seven and a half miles, shunting milk tanks as they went. This wonderful card, with the unmade road, the boys adorning the gateposts and the vintage rolling stock in the station, gives us a picture of the wayside station at its bucolic best. *(G Crease, Uffculme)*

62. Barnstaple already had a railway - the LSWR branch from Exeter - when the Devon & Somerset Railway built another one from Taunton in 1873. So, instead of getting one first-class railway, North Devon had to make do with two second-rate ones - both predominantly single-track and both served almost exclusively by stopping trains. By the time most passengers from Taunton got to **Swimbridge** their train would already have drawn up 12 times at places with names like Yeo Mill Halt and Venn Cross. This card was posted from Swimbridge in 1909, five years after the crossing loop and the platform on the right were built.

63. The GWR station at **Barnstaple** was a terminus from 1873 to 1887 when a spur was opened to the LSWR for trains to run through to Ilfracombe. It was renamed Victoria Road after nationalisation and closed to passengers in 1960, with Taunton-Barnstaple trains being diverted into the Junction station until they were withdrawn in 1966. Goods traffic continued to be handled at Victoria Road until 1970. Today, a relief road slices through the site and some of the buildings have been converted into a church.